Famous Legends

Pirate Legends

Gareth Stevens
PUBLISHING

By Jill Keppeler

Please visit our website, www.garethstevens.com. For a free color catalog of all our high-quality books, call toll free 1-800-542-2595 or fax 1-877-542-2596.

Cataloging-in-Publication Data

Names: Keppeler, Jill.
Title: Pirate legends / Jill Keppeler.
Description: New York : Gareth Stevens Publishing, 2018. | Series: Famous legends | Includes index.
Identifiers: ISBN 9781538202456 (pbk.) | ISBN 9781538203842 (library bound) | ISBN 9781538203835 (6 pack)
Subjects: LCSH: Pirates–Juvenile literature.
Classification: LCC G535.K47 2018 | DDC 910.45–dc23

First Edition

Published in 2018 by
Gareth Stevens Publishing
111 East 14th Street, Suite 349
New York, NY 10003

Copyright © 2018 Gareth Stevens Publishing

Designer: Laura Bowen
Editor: Therese Shea

Photo credits: Cover, p. 1 (pirates) SuperStock/Getty Images; cover, p. 1 (ribbon) barbaliss/Shutterstock.com; cover, p. 1 (leather) Pink Pueblo/Shutterstock.com; cover, pp. 1–32 (sign) Sarawut Padungkwan/Shutterstock.com; cover, pp. 1–32 (vines) vitasunny/Shutterstock.com; cover, pp. 1–32 (parchment) TyBy/Shutterstock.com; cover, pp. 1–32 (background) HorenkO/Shutterstock.com; p. 5 coniferine/Shutterstock.com; p. 7 (main) Silver Screen Collection/Moviepix/Getty Images; p. 7 (inset) Materialscientist/Wikimedia Commons; p. 9 Clausule/Wikimedia Commons; p. 10 Sergei Dvornikov/Shutterstock.com; p. 11 Film Favorites/Moviepix/Getty Images; p. 13 (portrait) OgreBot/Wikimedia Commons; pp. 13 (trial), 15 Print Collector/Hulton Fine Art Collection/Getty Images; p. 17 (flag) File Upload Bot/Wikimedia Commons; p. 17 (pirates) Print Collector/Hulton Archive/Getty Images; p. 18 Hulton Archive/Stringer/Getty Images; p. 19 Stefano Bianchetti/Corbis Historical/Getty Images; p. 21 (main) Marisa Estivill/Shutterstock.com; p. 21 (inset) Arcticpenguintours/Wikimedia Commons; p. 22 Rotational/Wikimedia Commons; p. 23 Joanna K-V/Shutterstock.com; p. 25 Fototeca Storica Nazionale/Hulton Archive/Getty Images; p. 27 (town and ships) Culture Club/Hulton Archive/Getty Images; p. 27 (portrait) King James of England/Wikimedia Commons; p. 28 Jack Jelly/Shutterstock.com; p. 29 Jesse Grant/Getty Images Entertainment/Getty Images.

All rights reserved. No part of this book may be reproduced in any form without permission in writing from the publisher, except by a reviewer.

Printed in China

CPSIA compliance information: Batch #CS17GS: For further information contact Gareth Stevens, New York, New York at 1-800-542-2595.

Contents

Ahoy, Matey! 4
On Treasure Island 6
Eye Patches, Peg Legs, and Hooks 8
Pirate Punishments 10
The Famous Captain Kidd 12
The Queen's Pirate 14
The Father of the Pirate Flag 16
Anne and Mary 18
On the China Sea 20
The Sea Queen 22
Blackbeard and Barbarossa 24
A Pirate by Another Name 26
The Legends Continue 28
Glossary 30
For More Information 31
Index 32

Words in the glossary appear in **bold** type the first time they are used in the text.

Ahoy, Matey!

Slowly, the tall ship slips across the sea. Its captain stands on the deck, a **treasure** map in one hand and a parrot on his shoulder. Overhead flies a black flag with a white **skull** and crossed bones. It's a pirate ship!

Pirate tales are very popular today, and many parts of these stories are real. Actual men and women sailed Earth's oceans, stealing from other ships and terrifying travelers. Each added to the exciting pirate **legends** we know today.

The Inside Story

Pirates are people who take part in piracy, or attacking and robbing ships on the open ocean. People love pirate tales—even though pirates weren't usually the good guys!

Talk Like a Pirate Day is September 19 each year. It's a fun time to say "Ahoy!" and "Arrr!" Real pirates probably didn't talk this way, though.

On Treasure Island

A lot of people's ideas about pirates come from Robert Louis Stevenson's *Treasure Island*, a book published in 1883. In it, a young man named Jim Hawkins joins a group of pirates looking for buried treasure. The leader of the pirates is named Long John Silver.

In the book, Silver has one leg and a pet parrot. Also, a treasure map has an X to mark where the riches are buried. These **details** are part of many popular pirate legends today.

The Inside Story

Stevenson may have based Long John Silver on actual men. Some historians think the pirate was modeled on real-life pirates Owen and John Lloyd of Wales.

Treasure Island has been made into many movies. One of the most famous was a 1950 movie in which actor Robert Newton starred as Long John Silver. He spoke in the way many think of as "pirate talk" today.

Robert Louis Stevenson

Eye Patches, Peg Legs, and Hooks

When people think of pirates, they might think of eye patches, **peg legs**, and hooks that replace hands. The life of a pirate was very dangerous. Pirates could lose body parts such as eyes, legs, and hands in battle, but also by doing tasks aboard a ship.

However, none of the most famous real-life pirates had peg legs or hooks. This picture of a pirate became common because of characters such as Long John Silver and Captain Hook from the Peter Pan stories.

The Inside Story

Some people think pirates might have worn eye patches because keeping one eye covered makes that eye get used to the dark faster. This is perfect when the pirate fights in the dark below deck!

Captain Hook first appeared in J. M. Barrie's play *Peter Pan; or, the Boy Who Wouldn't Grow Up* in 1904. He's appeared in many different **versions** of the story ever since.

Pirate Punishments

People say that pirates **punished** enemies by making them "walk the plank," or jump off a piece of wood at the side of a ship. This probably isn't true! That didn't stop people who wrote about pirate legends from saying it, though.

Real pirates were more likely to leave people on a deserted island. Or they might keelhaul them. This meant a person was hauled, or dragged, by a rope through the water and under the **keel** of the ship. Ouch!

If pirates really wanted to drown someone, all they had to do was throw them overboard. But walking the plank is a better story!

11

The Famous Captain Kidd

One of the most famous real pirates is William Kidd, who was born in Scotland about 1645. Kidd started as a privateer, which is a sailor who is paid by a government to attack and steal from enemy ships. Kidd often worked for Great Britain and its American colonies.

In 1698, Kidd and his crew attacked a ship full of treasure from India and took it over. People started saying he was a pirate. He was found **guilty** and put to death in 1701.

The Inside Story

Many people believe Captain Kidd buried treasure on one of the islands in the Caribbean Sea. It hasn't been found yet!

William Kidd is remembered as a very famous pirate today, but he tried to clear his name. He didn't want to be thought of as a pirate!

Captain William Kidd on trial

The Queen's Pirate

Many other pirates were like William Kidd, stealing with the support of their country's leaders. Queen Elizabeth I of England is said to have called explorer Sir Francis Drake "my pirate."

In 1577, Drake led only the second **voyage** to go all the way around the world and return to its starting point. Along the way, he also led many attacks against Spanish colonies and ships. By the time he returned home, he was a very rich pirate!

The Inside Story

Sir Francis Drake was called El Draque, or "The Dragon," by his Spanish enemies.

Queen Elizabeth knighting Drake

Drake was one of the Sea Dogs, the name for the privateers who attacked the Spanish for the British government.

The Father of the Pirate Flag

Everyone knows what it means when you see a ship flying a black flag with a white skull and crossed swords, or bones, on it. That means it's a pirate ship!

People used to call any pirate flag a "Jolly Roger." Each pirate used a different flag. According to legend, a pirate named John "Calico Jack" Rackham created the famous flag with the skull and swords. Calico Jack Rackham was captured in 1720 near the island of Jamaica. He was put to death not long afterward.

The Inside Story

Calico Jack wasn't a successful pirate. People remember him mostly because of his flag and two of his most famous sailors: Mary Read and Anne Bonny.

Calico Jack Rackham got his name because he liked to wear clothing made from calico, or a kind of cheap and often brightly colored cloth.

Anne Bonny, John "Calico Jack" Rackam, and Mary Read

Anne and Mary

Anne Bonny and Mary Read are two of history's most famous female pirates. They both served on the crew of Calico Jack Rackham. The women sometimes dressed as men when they were on board their ship. According to legend, both were strong, skilled fighters.

Bonny and Read were captured with the rest of Rackham's crew in 1720 and found guilty of piracy. Read died in prison, but stories say Bonny returned to her family in what is now South Carolina.

Mary Read and Calico Jack Rackham

Most of what people know about Bonny and Read comes from a book called *A General History of the Robberies and Murders of the Most Notorious Pyrates,* published in 1724.

On the China Sea

Not all pirates worked in the Caribbean. One of the most successful pirates in history was a woman who mostly sailed the China Sea. Cheng I Sao, or Ching Shih, commanded a **fleet** of more than 1,000 ships and thousands of pirates in the early 1800s.

Cheng I Sao started her path to piracy as the wife of a pirate named Cheng. When he died, she built her Red Flag Fleet into a fierce force that the Chinese government tried, but failed, to stop.

The Inside Story

Cheng I Sao had many rules for her pirates. If they didn't obey them, they could lose their ears—or their head!

Cheng I Sao in battle

Since the Chinese navy had no luck stopping Cheng I Sao, the government offered her a deal for peace. In 1810, she accepted it and **retired** from piracy.

The Sea Queen

Grace O'Malley was born about 1530 in Ireland. She became known as the Sea Queen of Connacht, an area in western Ireland. A member of a powerful Irish family, O'Malley controlled many ships. She and her crews attacked and robbed boats along Ireland's shores.

In 1593, when the British captured O'Malley's son and brother, she met with Queen Elizabeth I of Great Britain to ask for help. The queen freed her family, and Grace O'Malley continued to sail and lived to be more than 70 years old.

This tower at Kildavnet on Achill Island in Ireland is called Grace O'Malley's Castle. It's one of many tower houses she had built.

Blackbeard and Barbarossa

A couple of pirates got their names because of another common pirate feature: their beards! Blackbeard was a very famous pirate whose real name may have been Edward Teach. He led a large group of pirates in the early 1700s. They robbed ships throughout the Caribbean and near the southern coast of North America.

Barbarossa, which means "red beard" in Italian, is a name used by at least two brothers who were pirates near North Africa during the 16th century. The most famous is probably Hayreddin Barbarossa.

The Inside Story

Legend says Blackbeard set his long beard on fire during battles to scare his enemies!

Blackbeard likely burned pieces of rope he placed in his hair and beard, rather than his beard itself.

25

A Pirate by Another Name

"Buccaneer" is often used as another word for pirate, much like "privateer" is. But this isn't really what that word means. A buccaneer is a kind of pirate who attacked Spanish ships and towns in the Caribbean during the 1600s.

Henry Morgan was a very successful buccaneer during the 1660s and 1670s. He was born in Wales in 1635, but traveled to the Caribbean as a young man. There, he earned a name for himself as a pirate by attacking Spanish ships and settlements.

The Inside Story

After England and Spain made peace, Morgan was arrested. However, he was knighted by England's King Charles II in 1674 and returned to the Caribbean as a governor of Jamaica.

Henry Morgan is famous for **raiding** the city of Panama in 1671.

27

The Legends Continue

Pirates aren't usually on the side of the law. So why do people love them? Maybe it's because many people enjoy the idea of having adventures while sailing the ocean on a tall ship. Or maybe it's because everyone likes to imagine finding a mysterious map that leads to buried treasure.

Whatever the reason for their popularity, pirate stories and legends aren't going away soon. People continue to write books and make movies about pirates. Sometimes there's even a little truth in the tales!

Some of the most famous pirate stories are Disney's Pirates of the Caribbean movies. The idea for the movies came from the Pirates of the Caribbean ride at Disneyland in California and Walt Disney World in Florida.

actor Johnny Depp as Captain Jack Sparrow from the Pirates of the Caribbean movies

Glossary

detail: a small part of something

fleet: a number of ships under a single command

guilty: having committed, or done, a crime

keel: a long piece of wood running from front to back along the center of the bottom of a boat

legend: a story from the past that is believed by many people, but cannot be proved to be true

peg leg: a man-made leg, especially one that reaches only to the knee and is made of wood

punish: to make someone suffer for a crime

raid: to attack by surprise, often in order to steal

retire: to leave a job

skull: the boney frame of the head and face

treasure: wealth such as gold that has been stored away

version: a story that is different in some way from another telling of the story

voyage: a journey, especially by sea

For More Information

Books

Bearce, Stephanie. *Pirates and Buried Treasure: Secrets, Strange Tales, and Hidden Facts About Pirates.* Waco, TX: Prufrock Press, 2015.

Marsh, Carole. *The Mystery of Blackbeard the Pirate.* Peachtree City, GA: Gallopade International/Carole Marsh Books, 2010.

Rice, Dona Herweck. *Bad Guys and Gals of the High Seas.* Huntington Beach, CA: Teacher Created Materials, 2013.

Websites

Pirates
www.dkfindout.com/us/history/pirates/
This interactive website features a map of pirate activity.

Pirates! Fact & Legend
www.piratesinfo.com
Find out more pirate facts, including details about famous pirates, on this website.

Publisher's note to educators and parents: Our editors have carefully reviewed these websites to ensure that they are suitable for students. Many websites change frequently, however, and we cannot guarantee that a site's future contents will continue to meet our high standards of quality and educational value. Be advised that students should be closely supervised whenever they access the Internet.

Index

Barbarossa 24
Blackbeard 24, 25
Bonny, Anne 16, 18, 19
buccaneer 26
Captain Hook 8, 9
Cheng I Sao 20, 21
Drake, Francis 14, 15
Elizabeth I 14, 22
flags 4, 16
"Jolly Roger" 16
keelhauling 10
Kidd, William 12, 13, 14
Long John Silver 6, 7, 8
Morgan, Henry 26, 27
O'Malley, Grace 22

Pirates of the Caribbean movies 29
privateers 12, 15, 26
Rackham, John "Calico Jack" 16, 17, 18
Read, Mary 16, 18, 19
Sea Dogs 15
Stevenson, Robert Louis 6
Teach, Edward 24
treasure 4, 6, 12, 28
Treasure Island 6, 7
walking the plank 10, 11